5/11

DEMCO

Cool
SCHOOL
CLUBS

Karen Latchana Kenney

A Division of ABDO

ABDO
Publishing Company

visit us at www.abdopublishing.com

Published by ABDO Publishing Company, a division of ABDO, P.O. Box 398166,
Minneapolis, Minnesota 55439. Copyright © 2011 by Abdo Consulting Group,
Inc. International copyrights reserved in all countries. No part of this book
may be reproduced in any form without written permission from the publisher.
Checkerboard Library™ is a trademark and logo of ABDO Publishing Company.

Printed in the United States of America, North Mankato, Minnesota
112010
012011

 PRINTED ON RECYCLED PAPER

Editor: Liz Salzmann
Series Concept: Nancy Tuminelly
Cover and Interior Design: Anders Hanson, Mighty Media, Inc.
Photo Credits: Anders Hanson, Shutterstock, Thinkstock

The following manufacturers/names appearing in this book are trademarks:
Aleen's® Tacky Glue®, Elmer's® Glue-All™, Kittrich® Magic Cover®, Tulip® Crystals®

Library of Congress Cataloging-in-Publication Data

Kenney, Karen Latchana.
  Cool school clubs : fun ideas and activities to build school spirit / Karen Latchana
Kenney.
     p. cm. -- (Cool school spirit)
  Includes index.
  ISBN 978-1-61714-666-4
  1. Students--Societies, etc.--Juvenile literature. I. Title.
  LB3605.K39 2011
  371.8'3--dc22
                          2010024871

Contents

What's Cool About School Clubs?

Going to school is not just about homework and tests. You get to meet new friends and learn amazing new things. Plus there are so many activities to do and fun groups to join.

Being excited about school is your school spirit. One way to show it is by joining a school club. What do you love doing? Can you dance or sing? Or do you like to play games or learn languages? Guess what? School clubs are filled with other students who like doing the same things you do!

Joining a club is a way to make school cool! Learn about other **cultures** in a language club. Find ways to **recycle** in an environmental club. Or play chess in a club with your friends. If you want to show school spirit, joining a school club may be right for you!

Before You Start

It's a good idea to do some research before joining a club. Talk to club members and ask questions. Go to a few meetings and watch what goes on. See if the club is one you *want* to join and *can* join.

Time

- How often does the group meet?
- How long are meetings?
- Are there any trips required?

Skills

- What do members do at meetings?
- Do I need to have certain skills?
- How do I join the club?

Cost

- Do I need to pay a group fee?
- Are there trips or **tournaments** that have an extra cost?

Permission

Once you've done your research, check it out with your parents. Make sure you get permission to join the club. You may need a parent's help to fill out an application or registration form.

The World of School Clubs

When it comes to school clubs, you just have to choose! That can be difficult. There are many types of clubs to choose from. Here are just a few.

If you like to read, try a book club. Members read the same book before each meeting. Then at the meeting they discuss the story and its characters. It's a great way to get **motivated** about reading.

Chess is a game of logic and skill. Members of a chess club get together to play the game. As they get better, they might play in a **tournament**. This is when the club competes against other clubs.

Do you like learning languages? A language club would be great for you! Members learn to speak different languages. They also learn about **cultures** by cooking, playing games, and singing songs.

An environmental club is for kids who care about the earth. They learn about ways to **recycle** and be green. They also **volunteer** in the community to help the environment.

There are many other clubs to join at school. See what your school has to offer. The right club is waiting for you!

Way Back

Chess is the oldest game of skill. Each game piece is a symbol from **medieval** times. The pawns are symbols of the workers. The rooks are castles. The knights are the soldiers. And the bishops are symbols of the church. The queen is the most powerful piece. In medieval times, losing the king meant the end of the kingdom. That's why in chess losing the king means the game is over.

Tools & Supplies

Here are some of the materials you'll need to make the projects in this book!

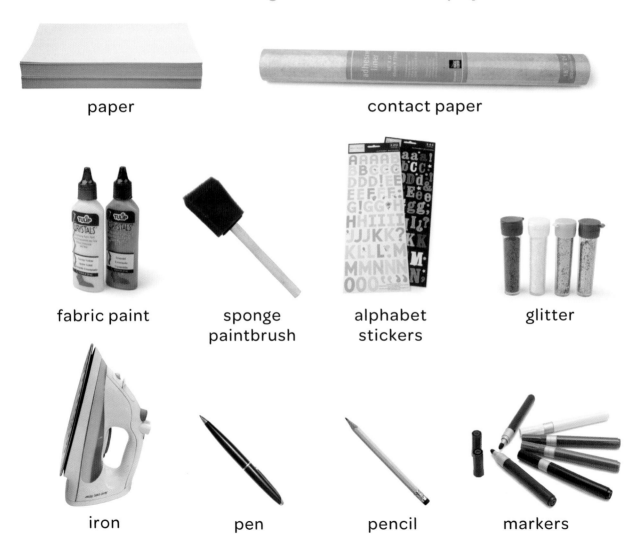

paper

contact paper

fabric paint

sponge paintbrush

alphabet stickers

glitter

iron

pen

pencil

markers

T-shirt

poster board

scissors

cardboard

clipboard

index cards

ruler

glue

colored paper

magazines

The Spanish Club Wants You!

Do you love Latin music or French food? You should join a language club! You'll learn a new language. And you'll learn about another **culture** too!

It's simple to join a language club. You just need to have an interest in joining. Find out when and where the club meets. Look for posters in your school. Listen for announcements. Then, show up for the next meeting!

Learning languages is a lot of fun! You can sing songs from other countries. And listen to different styles of music. Try reading fun stories in new languages. You can also make recipes from other countries. Put some of these things together, and have a language club party! It is a great way to get new members to join your club.

Great Guacamole!

Make this great guacamole for your Spanish club party! Mash two ripe avocados in a bowl. Chop up a fourth of a red onion and half of a bunch of cilantro. Stir them into the avocados. Squeeze the juice of half a lime into the bowl. To make it spicy, ask an adult to chop up a jalapeño and stir it in. Add a little salt and pepper. Serve it with a bowl of tortilla chips. Yum!

Host a Holy Guacamole Party!

Use fun posters to get a big crowd at your Spanish club party.

¿QUIEN (WHO)? **SPANISH CLUB**
¿DONDE (WHERE)? Cafeteria Friday after school
¿POR QUE (WHY)?
Eat our delicious top secret guacamole recipe... AND LEARN a salsa dance!

See you there!

What You'll Need

poster board, pencil, colored paper, scissors, markers, alphabet stickers, magazines, glue, glitter

1 **Brainstorm** ideas with club members about what to say on your poster. *What is the name of the party? When and where will the party be held? What will be fun about the party?* Write everyone's ideas down. Then vote on your favorites.

2 Think of images that have to do with your club. You can draw pictures, or cut them out of magazines. Use fun, colorful images!

3 Use a pencil to sketch on the poster board. Lightly mark where you will put the information. Decide where to put the pictures.

4 Glue the pictures onto the poster. Try gluing them on top of larger pieces of colored paper. Add glitter for decoration. Use alphabet stickers to spell out the name of the party.

5 Use markers to write the rest of the information. Make sure it's easy to read.

Go Team Green!

Is protecting the environment important to you? You can do your part to help. Why not get a whole team together? Your club can do even more for the earth!

An environmental club can do many things to help the earth. One way to help is to **inform** people about ways to **recycle**. Use posters to get the word out. Explain how to be green at home and at school. Find ways for your school to celebrate Earth Day.

Your club can also get out into the community and do work. Try cleaning a park or a block. Or help plant trees. **Volunteer** as a team. Everyone will **appreciate** your help!

These are big projects. And it takes teamwork to get things done. So it is important to get to know the other club members. Take time outside of club activities to have fun. You can play games or make **recycled** crafts! It's great being friends with the people in your club. It makes working together even better!

Environmental Experts

Each club member can become an environmental expert! Have each person research different ways to be green. Then have everyone share their research with the club. Knowing more will help your club **inform** other students. Try topics like recycling, keeping air and water clean, buying local, biking instead of driving, protecting animal **habitats**, and saving energy.

That's Not True!

This guessing game will help your club members be closer friends.

What You'll Need

index cards, pens

1 Give each club member an index card and a pen.

2 Ask everyone to think of two true facts about themselves. Then they should each think of a lie. The facts and the lie should be fun and unique!

3 Have each member write their facts and lie on their index card. They can write them in any order.

4 Collect the cards and give them to the club president or a teacher. Ask that person to read the cards aloud.

5 Time to guess! After each card is read, have the members try to guess who wrote it. See if anyone can tell which statement is not true. You'll learn a lot about the members of your club!

The Checkmate Champs!

Is your chess club going to a **tournament**? Looking like a team will make a big impression. Come up with a club logo. Then think of fun ways to show that you're a team!

Part of being in a chess club is playing with your team. Another part is playing in chess tournaments. You get to play against kids from other schools. Wouldn't it be fun to have a team shirt to wear?

18

A logo can help make you look like a team. A logo is a symbol that represents a group. Logos can have pictures and words, and the colors are important too. It is something that can be put on T-shirts or bags. A logo is also used on posters, banners, and other printed pieces.

The following activity will help you create a logo for your chess club. Be creative and make it look great. Then use it in different ways to represent your chess club!

Using Your Logo

When your logo is finished, scan it into the computer and save it as a picture. Use a document program to make things with your logo.

- Add it to letters

- Put it on flyers

- Print it on T-shirt transfer paper

If you can't use a computer, use a color copier. Make your logo as big or small as you want. Put it on banners, posters, and signs.

Make sure to keep the original logo safe. You'll want to use it again!

Look Good at the Chess Tournament!

Your chess club will look good with a new logo at your next tournament.

1 Start with a **brainstorming** session with your club. Ask questions such as *Should our logo have a theme? What words or letters should be in our logo? What picture should be in our logo? What colors should be in our logo?* Write everyone's ideas on a piece of paper.

2 Go through the list with the club. Vote for the best idea for each question and circle it.

3 Now sketch out your idea. Decide what shape you want your logo to fit inside. You could try a chessboard! Draw your shape on a piece of paper.

4 Put the picture and words inside the shape. You might need to make several sketches. Move the picture and words around. See what works best. Remember to keep it simple!

5 Show the sketches to your club. What do the other members think? Pick out the logo that everyone likes.

6 Now make a final sketch on a new piece of paper. Make the lines clear and sharp. This will help it look good whether it's printed big or small.

7 Color your logo with markers. Use only one or two colors. The colors should look clean and bright.

Bucks for the Book Club!

Did you know that you could help your club by reading? Raise money by having a **marathon**. Not a running marathon, but *reading* marathon! Just read as many books as you can!

A book marathon can be a kind of fund-raiser. It is a way to help your club raise money. The first step in fund-raising is setting goals. What are you trying to achieve? Do you need money for new books? Set your goal and then figure out how much money you need.

How are you going to raise funds for your club? There are many things you can do besides a book **marathon**. You can have a bake sale or sell used books. You can also make bookmarks to sell to parents and friends. **Brainstorm** ideas with the club. You may need to buy supplies. Include the amount you spend when deciding how much money you need.

During your fund-raiser, be friendly and show **appreciation**. Let people know how their money will help your club. They will be happy to help! And, don't be disappointed if your club doesn't make its goal. You tried and did your best!

Cool Bookmarks

Selling bookmarks can be a great way to raise money! Cut strips of colored paper. Put the book club's logo at the bottom. Find cool pictures to glue on the bookmarks. Or write fun book facts on the bookmarks. Put each bookmark between two pieces of clear contact paper. Then cut around the edges. Punch a hole in the top and tie on a ribbon.

Book Marathon!

Get sponsored to read and make money for your club!

What You'll Need

paper, pencil, ruler, markers, photocopier, clipboards

1 To get your book **marathon** started, you first need pledge sheets. Write your marathon's title at the top of a sheet of paper. Add a line for the reader's name. Use a pencil and ruler to divide the paper into five columns. Trace over the pencil lines with a marker.

2 Write a heading at the top of each column. The headings should be *sponsor name*, *phone/e-mail*, *pledge per book read*, *finished books*, *total donation*.

3 Draw a line under the headings using a pencil and ruler. Keep drawing row lines until the sheet is filled. Make photocopies of the pledge sheet. Give a sheet and a clipboard to each club member.

4 Tell members to ask friends and family to sponsor them for the marathon. They should explain how long the marathon lasts. Is it one day, one week, or even a month? Tell sponsors what the money will buy for the club.

5 The sponsors fill out the first three columns of the pledge sheet. The members keep track of the books they read during the marathon. When it is finished, members fill out the rest of their sheets. Then they call or e-mail their sponsors. Tell the sponsors the total of their donations. Explain how the money will be collected. And don't forget to thank them for helping the book club!

It's Good to Grow!

Does your club love to grow plants and flowers? Show it on a T-shirt you design yourself. Make one for each club member. Then wear them to school and show your spirit!

Green Thumbs Up!

Create cool T-shirts for your gardening club!

What You'll Need

contact paper, pencil, scissors, T-shirt, cardboard, fabric paint, sponge paintbrush, iron

1 Talk with the members of the gardening club. Decide on an image for your T-shirts. Do you grow vegetables or flowers? Or both? Pick an image that tells something about your club. Or spell out your club's name.

2 Use a pencil to draw the image on the contact paper. Just draw the outline. Do not put detail inside.

3 Cut the shape out of the contact paper. The paper will have a hole in the shape of your design. You will use it as a stencil.

4 Lay the T-shirt out flat. Place the shirt front side up. Smooth out any wrinkles.

5 Peel off the back of the contact paper. Press the stencil onto the shirt. Try to keep it smooth.

6 Put a piece of cardboard inside the shirt. It will stop the paint from soaking through.

7 Dab inside the stencil with paint. Use different colors or just one. Fill in the entire stencil.

8 Let the paint dry completely. Do not touch it or it could smear. It might take all night to dry!

9 Peel off the stencil. Turn the T-shirt inside out. Have an adult iron the back of where it was painted. This will help the paint set. Then try your shirt on. Looks great!

Sloatsburg Public Library
1 Liberty Rock Rd.
Sloatsburg, NY 10974

Conclusion

What do you love about school clubs? Is it the cool people you meet? Or is it the fun activities you are part of during the year? There are so many great things about being a member of a school club.

It is a way to support your school. And you meet people who like the same things as you. It's a great way to make friends and have fun. You get to achieve goals and participate in many different activities. This can help you become more confident outside of the club.

School clubs are one cool way to show your school spirit. But it is not the only way. Check out the other books in this series. Learn about other groups you can join at your school. Maybe you like to **volunteer** or dance. Or cheer for your school team as a cheerleader. There will be a group that fits your tastes. Take advantage of what your school has to offer. It is a great place to be!

Glossary

appreciate – to value or admire greatly.

brainstorm – to come up with a solution by having group members share ideas.

culture – the behavior, beliefs, art, and other products of a particular group of people.

habitat – the area or environment where a person or thing usually lives.

inform – to tell a person the facts known about an event or subject.

marathon – a game, contest, or other activity that takes a very long time.

medieval – of or belonging to the Middle Ages, a period of time from AD 500 to 1500.

motivated – to be interested or excited about doing something.

recycle – to process something so the materials it is made of can be used again.

tournament – a series of contests or games played to win a championship.

volunteer – to offer to do a job, most often without pay.

Web Sites

To learn more about cool school spirit, visit ABDO Publishing Company on the World Wide Web at **www.abdopublishing.com.** Web sites about cool school spirit are featured on our Book Links page. These links are routinely monitored and updated to provide the most current information available.

Index